64 MUSICAL STUDIES
for SAXOPHONE

Edited by

Dr. Rami El-Farrah

Copyright © 2020 Southern Music (ASCAP).
International Copyright Secured. All Rights Reserved.
Digital and photographic copying of this publication is illegal.

Contents

Foreword

64 Musical Studies for Saxophone is a compendium of Baroque, Classical, and Romantic-era masterpieces arranged for saxophone. The works are written to serve as a student primer to the *Ferling Studies* or other similar studies. Each lyrical study has been crafted to create a balance of musicality and pedagogy that allows students to improve on all aspects of performance. Players are encouraged to choose works that align with their musical goals, not necessarily in the listed order. Each piece is carefully formatted with style-appropriate dynamics, articulations, and tempos, all of which are carefully tailored to the saxophone. These musical studies give saxophonists the opportunity to experience compositions by Wolfgang Amadeus Mozart, Carl Philipp Emanuel Bach, Ernesto Köhler, Carl Maria von Weber, and many more.

Dr. Rami El-Farrah would like to thank Dr. Sunil Gadgil, Billyjon McPhail, Jessica Voigt Page, Ben Kessler, and Joshua Bryant for their support and commentary during the arrangement process. Immense gratitude and thanks goes as well to Dr. Si Millican for providing invaluable guidance and a true educator's perspective.

Dr. Rami El-Farrah is a concert saxophonist best known for his work as a soloist and member of the *Bel Cuore Quartet, Zenith Quintet,* and the *Austin Saxophone Ensemble.* As an award-winning soloist and chamber musician, he has performed across the United States and throughout Europe. El-Farrah has been featured on several musical albums, as well as new albums with *Bel Cuore Quartet* and *Austin Saxophone Ensemble.* In addition to concertizing, El-Farrah is a lecturer and instructs saxophone performance at The University of Texas at San Antonio, where he also directs the university's saxophone ensemble and teaches Jazz History.

As an arranger, Dr. El-Farrah is constantly creating new works for his ensembles and for other saxophonists across the U.S., many of which have performed and recorded his music. Other notable works by El-Farrah include *Dynamic Duos for Saxophone,* a two-part series for beginner/intermediate and advanced students of saxophone.

64 MUSICAL STUDIES
for SAXOPHONE

Edited by Dr. Rami El-Farrah

Moderato (♩ = 86)

Stanislas Verroust (1814-1863)

Moderato (♩ = 76)

Auguste Samie

B585

Andantino (♩ = 78)

Jules Demersseman (1833-1866)

3

Andante (♩ = 76)

Henri Kling (1842-1918)

4

Moderato e con Amore (♩ = 112)

Carl Maria von Weber (1786-1826)

8

Allegro (♩ = 112)

Xavier Désargus (1768-1832)

9

Ernesto Köhler (1849-1907)

Allegro (♩ = 120)

10

B585

10

Moderato (♩ = 86)

Théodore Botrel (1868-1925)

11

Allegretto (♩ = 100)

Marcia (♩ = 120)

Carl Maria von Weber (1786-1826)

12

Moderato quasi Andante (♩ = 82)

Richard Hofman (1844-1918)

13

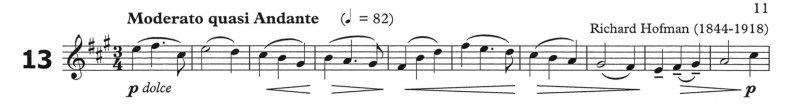

Allegro (♩ = 112)

Louis Adolphe Mayeur (1837-1894)

14

Allegro (♩ = 120)

Oskar Böeme (1870-1938)

15

Allegretto (♩ = 108)

Henri Kling (1842-1918)

16

Tempo di Minuetto (♩ = 92)

Carl Philipp Emanuel Bach (1714-1788)

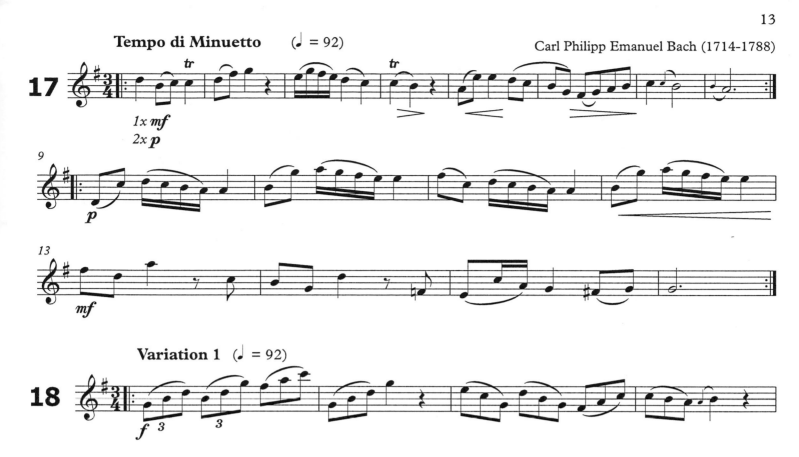

Allegro moderato (♩ = 116)

Ernesto Köhler (1849-1907)

20

p *dolce* *mp* *mp*

mf *p*

mp *p* *mf*

poco rit. *f*

a tempo

p *mp*

mp *mf* *rit.*

Moderato (♩ = 96)

Auguste Samie

21

p *sf*

sf *cresc.* *p*

Fine

f *p*

D.C. al Fine

p *mp* *f*

La Dragonne

Traditional Irish

Moderato (♩ = 98)

Auguste Samie

Allegretto bien décidé (♩. = 108)

Théodore Botrel (1868-1925)

B585

Oiseaux, Si Tous Les Ans
Ariette

Wolfgang Amadeus Mozart (1756-1791)

27

Les Capacins Maidons

Traditional Irish

28

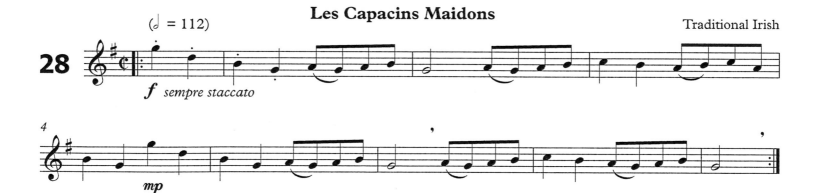

Rondo - Vivace ($\dot\downarrow$ = 126)

John Grimshaw (1765-1819)

29

Moderato ($\downarrow$ = 96)

Henri Kling (1842-1918)

30

Andantino sostenuto (♩. = 56)

Richard Hofman (1844-1918)

31

p espressivo

p — *cresc.*

mf — *p* — *f*

dim.

a tempo

p — *rit.* — *p* — *mf*

f

p — *mf* — *mp*

Allegretto (♩ = 104)

Théodore Botrel (1868-1925)

32

mf — *p* — *mf*

Fine

p — *mf*

p — *mp* — *mf*

D.C. al Fine

f

Colonel Tarleton's Quick March

Traditional Irish

(♩ = 92)

33

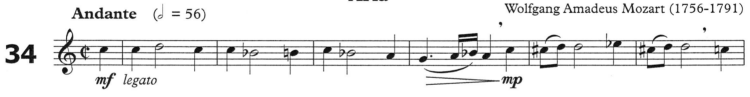

Se ardire, e speranza
Aria

Wolfgang Amadeus Mozart (1756-1791)

Andante (♩ = 56)

34

Au fond du fifre

Xavier Désargus (1768-1832)

(♩. = 88)

38

Rondo - Vivace (♩ = 112)

John Grimshaw (1765-1819)

39

Fine

D.S. al Fine

Theme with Variations

Theme - Andante ($\quad$ = 80)

Thomas Lindsay Willman (1784-1840)

Variation 6 (♩ = 80)

Andante (♩. = 63)   Giovanni Luca Conforti (1560-1608)

Fine

D.C. al Fine

La Tempest   Traditional Irish

(♩ = 116)

Menuet & Variations (♩ = 104)

John Stanley (1712-1786)

26

49

1st Variation (♩ = 104)

50

2nd Variation (♩. = 104)

51

3rd Variation (♩ = 104)

52

Allegretto (♩ = 108)

Giovanni Luca Conforti (1560-1608)

53

Aria - Andante con moto (♩ = 76)

August Kühnel (1645-1700)

Variation 1 - Allegretto (♩ = 108)

Variation 2 - Allegro (♩ = 112)

Allegretto vivo (♩. = 120)

Ernesto Köhler (1849-1907)

57

p

cedez en peu

dim.

a tempo

p

mf

rall.

Andante con moto (♩ = 66)

Théo Charlier (1868-1944)

58

f

mf

p

p dolce

March of the 17th Regiment

Traditional Irish

59

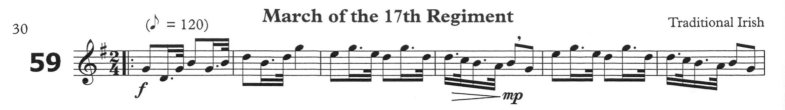

Andantino ($\eighthnote$ = 120)

Stanislas Verroust (1814-1863)

60

B585

Moderato (♩ = 86)

Giovanni Luca Conforti (1560-1608)

61

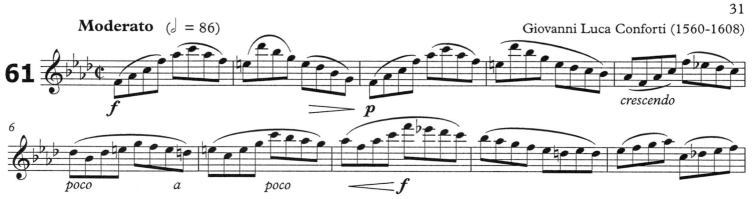

f

crescendo

poco   a   poco   *f*

p

mp

mf

sub. p   *crescendo   poco   a   poco*   *f*

Largo (♪ = 86)

Carlo Paessler (1774-1865)

62

p dolce   *mp*

mf   *p*

afflitto   *mp*   *mf*

a tempo

cresc.   *f*   *allargando*   *p con affetto*

mp dolce   *con forza*

f   *p*